TOOLS FOR TEACHERS

- **ATOS:** 0.6
- **GRL:** B
- **WORD COUNT:** 23

- **CURRICULUM CONNECTIONS:** transportation

Skills to Teach

- **HIGH-FREQUENCY WORDS:** go, the, to
- **CONTENT WORDS:** across, around, over, station, through, trains, under
- **PUNCTUATION:** periods
- **WORD STUDY:** /oo/, spelled ou (through); /ow/, spelled ou (around); /sh/, spelled ti (station)
- **TEXT TYPE:** factual description

Before Reading Activities

- Read the title and give a simple statement of the main idea.
- Have students "walk" though the book and talk about what they see in the pictures.
- Introduce new vocabulary by having students predict the first letter and locate the word in the text.
- Discuss any unfamiliar concepts that are in the text.

After Reading Activities

Trains go through, over, under, and around. Explain to children that directionals are adjectives. They tell us how or in which direction something moves. Can they name other ways in which trains might move? Forward? Backward? Write their answers on the board. What other vehicles can make these same movements?

Tadpole Books are published by Jump!, 5357 Penn Avenue South, Minneapolis, MN 55419, www.jumplibrary.com

Copyright ©2019 Jump. International copyright reserved in all countries. No part of this book may be reproduced in any form without written permission from the publisher.

Editor: Jenna Trnka **Designer:** Anna Peterson

Photo Credits: frontpoint/iStock, cover; aapsky/Shutterstock, 1; Tomas Kulaja/Shutterstock, 2–3; Pavliha/iStock, 4–5, 16tr; Kevin George/Alamy, 6–7, 16br; Kevin Klarer/Shutterstock, 8–9, 16tm; Modfos/Dreamstime, 10–11, 16bm; Gregory_DUBUS/iStock, 12–13, 16tl; Richie Chan/Shutterstock, 14–15, 16bl.

Library of Congress Cataloging-in-Publication Data is available at www.loc.gov or upon request from the publisher.
978-1-62496-997-3 (hardcover)
978-1-62496-998-0 (paperback)
978-1-62496-999-7 (ebook)

LET'S GO!

TRAINS

by Tessa Kenan

TABLE OF CONTENTS

tadpole
books

TRAINS

train

Trains go.

Trains go over.

6

Trains go under.

Trains go around.

Trains go through.

Trains go across.

station

Trains go to the station.

WORDS TO KNOW

across

around

over

station

through

under

INDEX